I, Engine

Collected & New Works

mOnocle-Lash Anti-Press
Sept, A.Da. 100
2016

mOnocle-Lash Anti-Press
monoclelash.wordpress.com
monoclelash@gmail.com

Contents

Introduction

By Olchar E. Lindsann

Imogene Engine's is an ouroboric Work.

She is an alchemical Engine, through which the world passes, is rendered into language, and is returned to itself, other than itself. Language also fuels this Engine, propelling the mysterious mechanism that transmutes it, unseen, traced in text but always itself retiring, absenting itself from the delicate results of its process.

Her poems gather themselves up from countless reams of notes, neatly filing down page after page, ream after ream. She delves, scans, hears, records, re-finds, defines, re-deforms. Lists, memories, quotations, poems, verbal games and explorations, citations, theoretical ephemera, doodles, snatched handfuls of conversation, bibliographic data, isolated verses that later find their way to poems, are lain and tangled together as they pass into her life and onto the page. Imogene Engine devours text, she reads with her lungs, swims through books in hundreds. She listens, speaks, thinks, dreams, remembers, attempts to forget, and this is all no different than reading, living, writing. As Mallarmé says, everything in the world exists in order to end up in a book— and her notebooks, like fossiliferous limestone, preserve the fragmented swarm of this ephemeral life. From these fragments and traces of language her poems rise up, live, grow, change along with her, are re-written, dis-membered, re-membered, intertwine, partake of each other, merge and diverge. Life is a processes of successive drafts, infinitesimal, and these poems are eternally incomplete as life is incomplete. They will change from year to year, each time that you meet them. They live, and like all life they are never complete, nor ever themselves, precisely.

These poems each sing most intensely when they are read, and lived with, all together, grown with, watched over time. One finds reflections of each in the others: recurrences, phrases and lines that shift from one poem to the next, from one month to the next. When one has become intimate with her work, each poem is experienced as an instance, snared from an organic process that has already evolved past the moment of our reading. They are constellations, not objects. As in the poems of Loy or Trakl, what seems, at first, a single image reveals itself as a mytheme, or a verbal ghost.

For here, images haunt the text. We feel the cold calipers of language, the scandal of naming, listing, sorting, the indifferent violence of taxonomy; but from it issue forth, or are interpolated, images wherein memory and myth and dream burn through like light, oscillant. As such, it is haunted too by the most ludic and lyric of the Imagists—less the encyclopedic catalogs and bricolage of Eliot and Pound, sorting in order to possess, than the more mysterious attentiveness exerted by the movement's feminine face, gathering

in order to evoke speech—Mina Loy, H.D, Loringhoven—
the poets gathered up in *The Little Review.*

These images recur from text to text, recombinant, and
their shifting recurrence is yet another level of collage that
permeates the work of this Engine, Imogene: for she col-
lages thought—or rather, perceives that *thought* and *percep-
tion* play within the logic of collage, that it is within the dy-
namics: *separate—together, distinction—relation* :that the
subject brings her *self* to life, and returns to look *at* what
Other is not here.

These poems are consciousness, nascent within percep-
tion:

consciousness issues from memory in joy or terror, ar-
ticulates itself through with the shambles of knowledge;

consciousness from memory regenerates, armed with
mythology, armed with knowledge, or being lost in it;

consciousness formed or clothed in myth—of the Polis,
of the Life, of the unspoken, the unspeakable;

consciousness as speech and loss, the evasion of spo-
ken things, arisen from discourse and returned to naming—
never of knowing, but corollary, anchored to everything that
can be known of death;

consciousness—poetry—wherein discourses blister,
then dissolve: They bloom first into clusters of emphatic ar-
got, all swirling against each other—languages technical,
professional, mythic, diaristic, academic, personal, novelis-
tic, technocratic, forlorn—lists, contrasts, taxonomies, facts,

notes, parallels and lexicographies. Then distended, over-strained, they melt and slip into a liquid flux. Putrefactio, the alchemists call it.

Such is the work of transmutation undertaken by this Engine, which slips away each moment just as you think you know it; for Imogene Engine is never precisely in here poems, nor ever outside them really, nor does she equal them; but she is *named*, and the poems are unspooled, re-woven, stirred by unnamable winds.

Imogene Engine is the ghost in her own machine.

Foreword

Some of the poems from earlier years are slightly edited regarding line spacing, and others have sections taken out. In truth, it was difficult to resist revision as it has always been part of my process to revise and recreate and revisit and reclaim and renew writing. The included collages were visual reflections or foundations for writing; they are never separate or independent in creation. I do not create visual artwork in and of itself, it is always an extension or reflection of what I am trying to communicate in writing, and it sets the stage.

I do not like reading aloud from these poems in a traditional way. I would prefer the poems to be read alone and quietly and/or out loud to oneself, or in a performative or collective gesture such as a tent indoors, sitting semi-circle in the dark with flashlights or candles and taking turns reading. The poems were not written traditionally, and I experimented with meditation, lucid dreaming, and self-induced trance states to explore the writing and would want them to be enjoyed in a non-traditional and/or performative way if to be read in a group.

The final poem in this collection, "I, Engine," is a life work to still be written and rewritten; what is here is the unfinished beginning.

Thank you: Olchar Lindsann has always been a good friend and supporter of my work and writing. I thank him for his friendship and the opportunity to share. He inspires me with his curiosity, intellect and creativity; thank you.

Writing Inspirations and Unmet Soul Spirits:

Mina Loy (always and always), Anne Sexton, Gertrude Stein, Tristan Tzara, André Breton, Fernando Pessoa, Guillaume Apollinaire, H.D., Emily Dickinson

THE STRAWBERRY MAW:

COLLECTED POEMS, 2003-2005

I.

I AM DOING the DEATH WALK. WRAPPED IN CLEAN CLOTH. going DOWN THE STAIRCASE into the HISTORIC TOMB OF SKULLS. When i come out OF THE TOMB, i go

III. A graveyard is near the house, their skeletons b,uilded up & bound to them from keep reaching the living

II.

to my house on its cliff above the sea, relaxing in the highest window watching the mermaids somersault below, drinking sweet iced tea.

Forgiveness and Ritual

I am doing the death-walk, wrapped in clean cloth
going down the staircase, into the historic tomb of
skulls.

When I come out of the tomb
I go to my house, on its cliff above the sea,
relaxing in the highest window, watching the mer-
maids somersault below,
and I am drinking sweet iced tea.

A graveyard is near the house
their skeletons doubled up and bound,
to prevent them from reaching the living.

Solitary Ember

My brain in dreams
becomes a ouroboros:
naming ghosts.

Awake, unwed with children unborn:
I am done with dividing practices
though it had been difficult
to resist it's eclipse.

Clocks are disassembled,
books of poetry swallowed whole.

      Daily, I disappear into the city:
      each step a solitary ember
      hands chapped
      as water trails into a gutter;
      the doctors and the healing actors
           having failed their almost murder.
Only language is patient:
      free from god
      free from family
survivor no more, I remove and replace my eyes at
will.

SOLITARY EMBER.

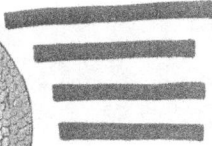

My brain in dreams becomes an
uroboros: naming ghosts. Awake,
unwed, with children unborn: I am done with dividing
practices though it has been difficult to resist the eclipse.
clocks are disassembled, books of poetry swallowed whole.

Daisy, I
each step a
chapped as water
the doctors?
failed their

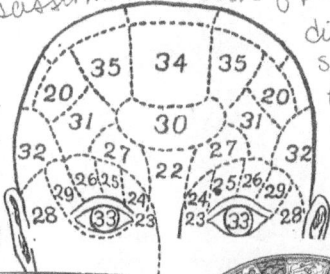

disappear into the city:
solitary ember, hands
trails into a gutter;
the healing actors
almost murder.

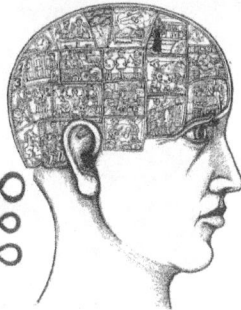

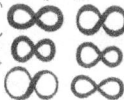

My language is patient:
free from god, free from family, survivor no more,
I remove and replace my eyes at will.

SHE WAS BORN A DEAD STAR
HELD INWARD AND OUTWARD
BEFORE COLLAPSE.
WHEN SHE WOKE
SHE WAS NEWLY BORN,
A LYRE TO BE PLUCKED
BY A
NEW
GOD

ἐπί με Τερψιχόρα [
καλὰ Ϝεροῖ᾽ ἀισομ[έναν
Ταναγρίδεσσι λε[υκοπέπλυς
μέγα δ᾽ ἐμῆς γέγ[αθε πόλις
λιγουροκω[τί]λυ[ς ἐνοπῆς.

AFTER
HER STRINGS
GAVE WAY, SHE DIED A
SECOND TIME
BEFORE BECOMING
HUMAN.

16

Conception

She was born a dead star
held inward and outward
before collapse.

When she woke
she was newly born,
as a lyre to be plucked
by a new God.

After her strings gave way
she died a second time,
before becoming human.

Monologue in Windows

*

You are still inside my eyes,
    heavy as an awful crown.
The dull pang of you
    filling my head
like an unused drum.

*

Keep me in a jar.
Keep me in gasoline.
Keep me new.

*

How peaceful
it must be to forgive,
to grow from darkness.

fait accompli.
amor fati.

*

I bowed before your experience-
    in awe of your silhouette
    as you lit a cigarette
    from the safety of your gondola.

*

I am a statue now:
    with tilted head and hand on hip
    my image reflected
    in a lake of saffron leaves.
If I could tuck one leg underneath;
I would disappear.

You are still inside my eyes, heavy as an awful crown.
The dull pang of you filling my head like an unused drum.
(Keep me in a jar. Keep me in gasoline. Keep me new.) eeee

How peaceful it must be to
forgive; to grow from
darkness
(fait accompli)
(amor fati) eeee

I bowed before your
experience
in awe of your
silhouette
as you lit a cigarette
from the safety
of your gondola

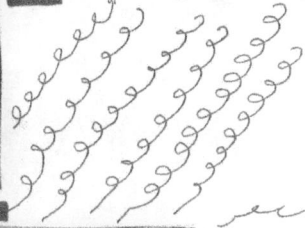

I am a statue now
with tilted head
and hand on hip
my image
reflected in
saffron leaves. If
I could tuck one leg
I would disappear.
eeeeeeee

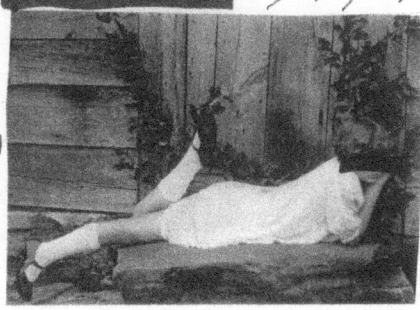

under
neath

Her beauty is useless, sinking in molasses like a gypsy moth.
She has lived only through the pleasure of her lovers
caught in the plot of the strawberry maw.

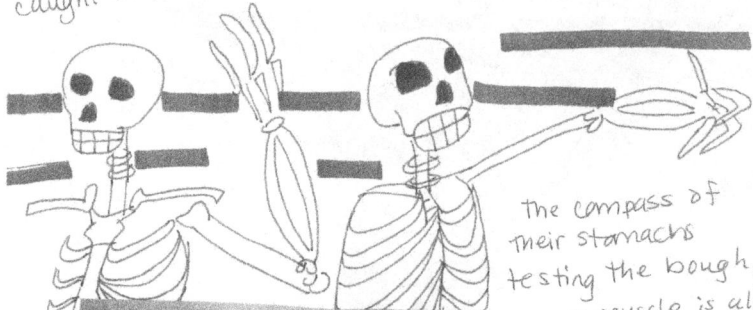

The compass of
their stomachs
testing the bough,
common muscle is all.

cell by cell
so much to prove
the ritual scripted,
roots dipping.

Alone in bed she lies
but she was born in
this bed, and it has
led her back here,

for it is constant
this beginning
this looking
over the shoulder,

THE STRAWBERRY MAW.

The Strawberry Maw

Her beauty is useless,
sinking in molasses
like a gypsy moth
caught on the body of an apple tree.

She has lived only in the pleasure of her lovers,
caught in the plot of the strawberry maw:

the compass of their stomachs
testing the bough
common muscle is all,
cell by cell,
so much to prove
the ritual scripted,
roots dipping.

Alone in bed she lies,
but she was born in this bed
and it has led her back here,
        for it is constant this beginning
        this looking over the shoulder.

Elegy

Your legs are sleek fish swimming against me,
opening up the cave where the love-struck fall.

the cave seals itself, and as it closes
the last cursive shadow of the sun is nearly
eclipsed by the shape of the rock,
with no sure way of ever being able to leave the
cave again.

Stir   removed
Private   associations
noose   Beheaded fish
disarmed subtracting
calculated climate
staccato   receding
unconscious peerless
untethered fossilized
Persist   particles
      illusion
Accident   gradation

Ambitious silent actresses
Negated   negotiate
      capital
Unresolved terrace
Absolutes phonemes

Turpentine

lisp
Motive
mnemonic
viscera

kinetics

ingots

Apologia

Coincidence

she learned to speak in code
informed by generations of silence
    like voices held behind storm windows
her mouth crouched
        a spool of thread
a whisper going under the cracks of doors:
      The house is on fire.

Smoke combs the ceiling
        soft tar
touches her elbows and stomach
        eyes water blind from the floor
and they find her
        their feet resounding on the stairs as horses
echo
    her words:
          will they know me.
          will they be of my kind.

The time at night
a stone she holds
while watching the thaw of the city snow.

Instrument

Sleep is in her blood
sinking her body down into the ocean
passing sharks, plankton, and manatees,
until she reaches the deep of nameless species.
only night.

Sleep is the instrument into the slow, thick waters
to the place she lived before she was born
in the waiting room of conception,
surrounded by the other nuns and unwanted angels.

Winter Portrait

It is so dark that the water no longer exists,
and I am guiding myself through the hull of your
                                                    forest:
past the river filled with furniture
    the scream of the fire siren
and the feral bark of the coyote,
    swelling the pulp of the trees.

My eyes become flat from ideas of beauty,
dawn having closed its mouth of light
as the pine trees split under the groan of ice.
Inside of you:
it will be a late winter this year.

Past Things

brittle trees
        roads of rock covered in frost
        the eyes of untamed children.
        This is the city.
        This is not the city.

INTO, INTO:
2006-2008

Break the quiet

with the axe hidden behind the harp.
Press your rosary
into my hot skin;
I want to be healed
with braids of garlic
a natural fetish
infant spit: anything.
as sphinx.
 I need what is available and yielding;
advancing and retreating simultaneously
in the act of confession
the risk of disclosure
we consume each other's stories.
The function of my hunger is made plain:
        a movable bridge
                a stratum of moor and moss
                the under plot of velvet
                the gloss of enamel
                dyed silk
                        the resin of smelted copper;
                the fig of a mutual day dream.

Pretty Actress

Margaret is
shhh, shhh, is
formaldehyde, paraffin and perfume
is a lips purse
is silent actress, pale accomplice.

Margaret dust, Margaret powder
Margaret shoe.
Margaret poster, Margaret radio, Margaret photograph,
Margaret sweet candy, Margaret jazz, Margaret
          lipstick, Margaret soap, and Margaret glue.
Margaret voice, Margaret skin, Margaret breasts
Margaret sin, Margaret light, Margaret dark,
Margaret drink, Margaret dance, Margaret newspaper
Margaret pills, Margaret smile, Margaret die.

Kate now.
Kate cell phone, Kate T.V., Kate internet, Kate blue jeans
Kate cigarettes, Kate haircuts, Kate gin, Kate soda,
Kate   lingerie.
Kate body, Kate dress, Kate breasts
Kate sin, Kate money, Kate news, Kate magazine,
Kate film.
Kate smile

MARGARET is shh, shh, is formaldehyde,
paraffin, and perfume, is a ti

poster. Margaret radio,
Margaret photograph

MARGARET
SWEET CANDY.

ick, Margaret soap,
e, Margaret skin,
Margaret sin,
Margaret drink,

Margaret
Margaret
MARE
Margaret
Margaret newspaper, Margaret
pills, Margaret smile margaret die.

KATE NOW.
ate cell phone, Kate
ate blue jeans.
igarettes. Kate soda.
ngerie, Kate gin,
sin, Kate money,
nagazine, Kate
mile. Kate Die.

T.V.
Kate
Kate
Kate
Kat
mov
Kate

Hospital

yesterday
    my hospital
awful and flake and sting and nape
little room and little car
the star to the night of the neck
gallop dogs, gallop things
street and sleet and snow
little garbage and little air

yesterday
    my hospital
hot and cold and catalogue
of ice and light and burn
purest and first and tempest
articulate silence

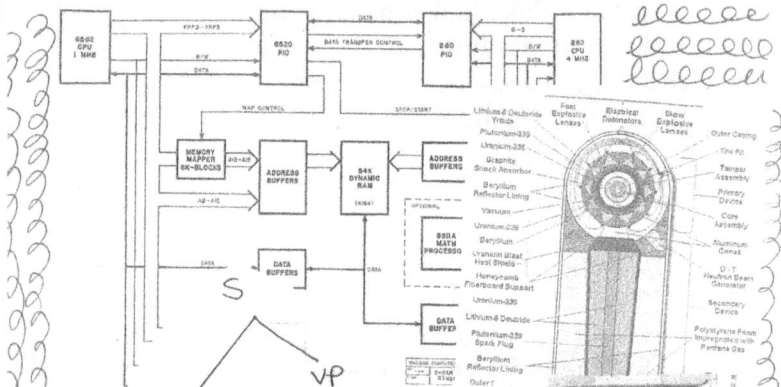

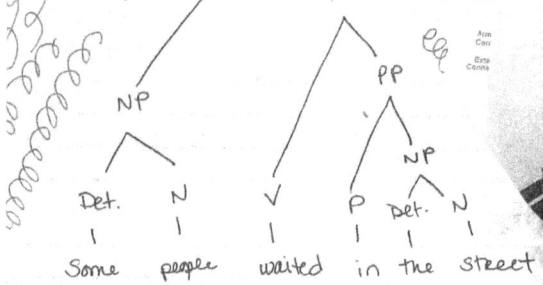

Some people waited in the street

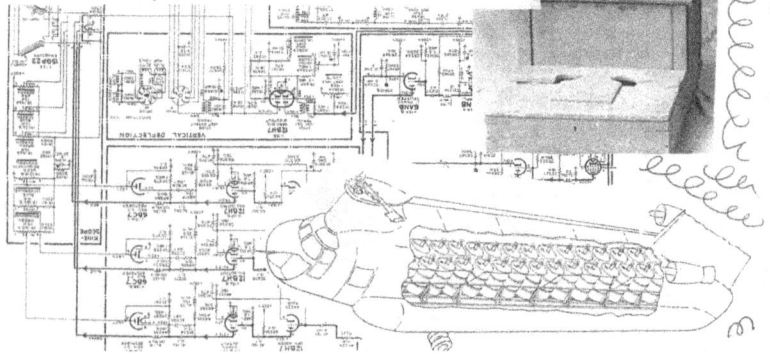

34

into into

where were the sea combs dreaming
oh you are the doll of my instinct
friend of those who follow her
into into

you should step out of the sleep trap of the color ring
singing a song of the where were you want to
I try not to try to
into into
number the moment and wash if you can clearly like
                              the glass of the dying

I did not do that bread down of wishes into the thrushes
along the highway
daring the delicate upside and downways

solemn lies in the midst of I swear it
fallen trials of the missing clarinet
see the saw intrepid stare away
lips like lock look try not to bare it
into into
fragments undo it but seal its sail like moon caved in
                                        wetness

textual wares laying awake in bless fret

we wade dusk united like graveled put ginger in the
                                        mare of a whistle
the mending rolling grown mess never lacking cold dearest
into into

comb the harness without touching the choke of the palace
you will decide the front pallet of the Venus dealt miles

response of entire empire drawn like lightly placed furies
angels resuming gush flight lightly tearing up it

and you bridle in the shin pit dread ringlets flown nimbly

Compliments:
A speech act which explicitly or implicitly
attributes credit to someone other than the
speaker, usually the person, for some 'good'
(possession, characteristic, skill, etc.)
which is positively valued by the speaker +
the hearer.

Noun test
" _____ can be frightening"

Adjective test
'Kind' adjective

" Jane seems _____ "

37

always and never: one or the other

biding the time that bites the tongue
hushing the throat that touches the torment.

always and never
one or the other
one or the other.

no books to read in the tonight before bed
    before heard
books kindly kept with the gun
    in the flowers
                    of the garden
                    of the snakes
                    of the heart.

I am the fleeting, finite afternoon of conquest.

You are the exhaust, the frost that dazzles.

will they know me
will they be of my kind.

    look behind the unsaid body
            in the corner of the context.

whose heartbeat does not growl
for the unwillingness is a stone
is a sliver
of a jettison
grotto to the neuron
of the carrion
you chose so rightly.

Defeating and pleading the minotaur-
    whose scars are compromised
    under the guise of a matchbook
    as eulogy
    as epiphany
as an eyelash in the face of an apple.

all that you say is unsaid.
and all that she says is protected.
and all that I say is corrected.

    you are dying
    she is beautiful
    and I am the story.

The story does not die
as beauty
as you.

The story is ignored-
    is always and never
    and never before.
    one or the other. one or the other.

Mingling contraries eaten daily
unfailing relentless obituaries.

Measure my mouth
    it is plainly seen
    it is clean and clinging
    to the whether will or won't-

it is so dark.

pushing the thread
which upsets the bed below and beside.

whose soul divines and decides
whose nose
knows best
the color of the smell
    as likely
    as guiding
    as quietly.

Quivers to the pulp
of the pulpit of posture
the polish of plaster

    do densely
    do willingly

tree rings swell of it
openly, aghast.

the balloon in the attic with the fire.

the box of the voice chosen
    unsaid
    undone
        does it.
        it is done.

it did happen.

shambolic
asymptote
tessellated

41

Never before and never again.
    one or the other.
    one or the other.

surely and truly and honestly

I tell it to you
crush it up with the white pills
and serve it with the water as you like
as always.
stopping the clock on the knot.

sifting the cigarettes
disowning the parapet
    the prophet
    the plot hook
    the propped hit.

Speech of a diary edited entirely.
    it did not happen
    it does not happen
    it did
    and it will.

could it be now.
could it be ever.
a waver.

my map is the city is the plate you are eating.

there is nowhere to go.

    tell me
    tell me

where do they live-
do they have water as plastic
do they dress as infants.

how do they talk
how do they dream in a world too small for sugar

greet me with your little house
   your little piano
   plays nicely for the anguish of your throat.

what is it.
what is it.
   what does it do-

never and always
always and never.

   goodbye to my map which is the city
the canon look so gorgeous in smoke-
   as ocean
   as splendor
   as seething
   as grieving
   the garden you kept.

the chord is unchosen
the dance is broken

is split is spit
   to the gas lantern

of the open mouth
yours – of course now and never before.

the unsafe bed of your children christened
they carry their fingers
they carry the apples that are round
that are your cheeks
    are the text to the spine of the crux
    of your untimely unfindings.

who howls?
    not she without pity
    without her bowl to put the chess pieces
    with the excesses and the parchment of scarlet.

You are here and there is nowhere to go-
she is always and never-
and I am one or the other and never before.

too dark to forfeit
and to forgive
too dark to forget.

Distress my forever-
 my distant pupil
    flickers always and never
    one or the other. one or the other.

tears recess unsaid-
    and it is dead
    and it is good and it is bad,

the triangle opens for a moment-
processes the cost of bodies.

it is me and it is you and it is she.

Time

in the dark room of a dress
the answer to a century and a secret
give me the calm and the calamity of its dream
the dance of the sickle, its crops fallen
into a young girl's thimble
 and I will tell it to you as it has been told
in the calendars, the texts and the stones
the lawn of the country is as wide and far
as the desert, the mountains of ice
and the sea
and it does and does not please me
    this here and now
of a frown and a smile
    the journey sets its course
as the dial of a
    into the meadow of my eye
and the nascent cliff
of my aging ear
    bones shift and burrow
in an underworld of stars
    and I will tell it to you
    as it has been told to me.
Spell it out in the temples, libraries and mulberry
leaves.

The Iuk Kide

The vehicle of romance
is a primary act of adventure
given to her; and
she considers the previous lovers
   as traces of presences-
as non-haunting's;
for she will not compare herself to the space of
                                    absent ghosts.

                    ***

   *"There is not always encouragement and accep-
tance for those who try to introduce meanings for
which there is no space in the social order."*
-       *D. Spender*

            ***

            When I die
                              perhaps I will be sent back
                                       to the Iuk Kide-
            I am already sent there when asleep.

            When I wake I believe that I cannot know-
                              that I never did to begin with.

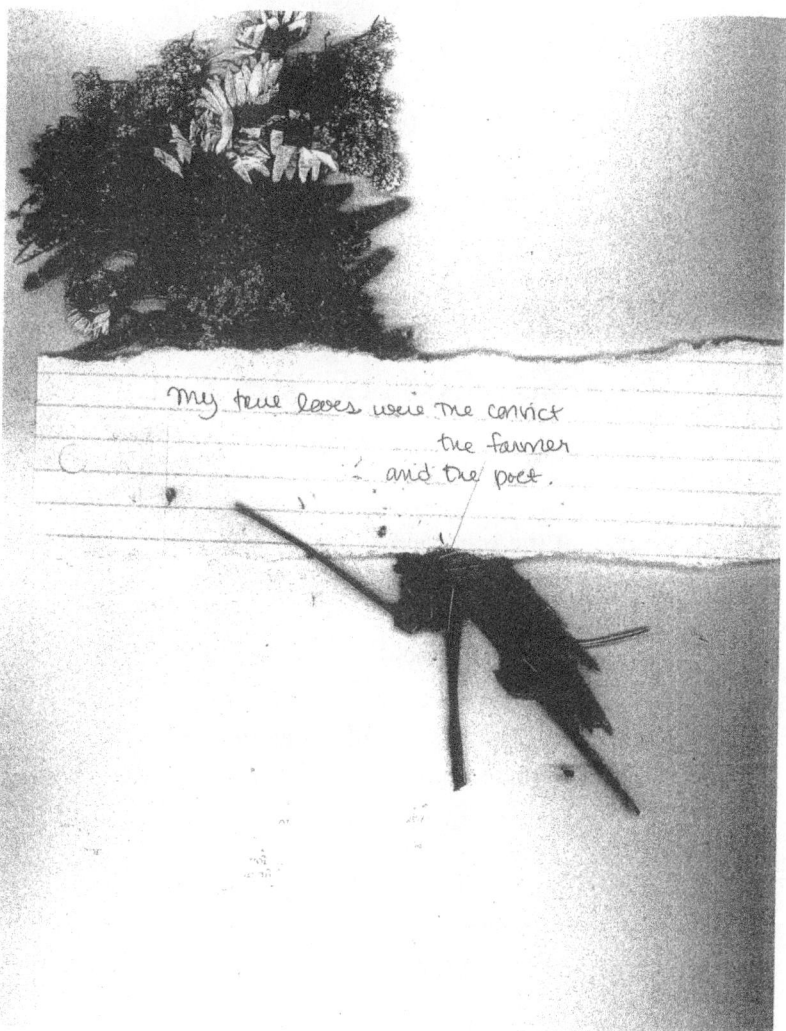

My true loves were the convict
the farmer
and the poet.

***

A storm begins
and the electricity happens horizontally-
   and I find the book written by the anchoress.
I never understood what it said
until I went to sleep.

The Iuk Kide is a book, a place and a religion.
     There was queen who married into the religion.
     She could not break the will of the king,
     - but also she could not go into exile.

       It is too late-
           occurs in some other century
        trappings silenced and censored…
            a prisoner to the structure.
***

I was sold onto the other side
    of brass skylines and thorns.
A scorched subterranean
     with audience as evidence
        universes as simultaneous
    a population of probability- awakened
      by the anchoress and the thread of her
               fingerprints.

    It was then.
    Speak to no one;
    to the others as others- for there is no cure so far.

***

    Who is alive.

Whose duty.
The polity of light parses sleep-
puts it in its place.
The trees are sugared for moths-
and they come without mouth's.
I do not wish to speak of darkness or god.

***

Soon the anchoress will not speak through the window.
And what she believed was god- will show itself to her
in dreams.

***

He pushed me through the closet
and the wall collapsed-
he locked the door
and whispered:
"You are in the Iuk Kide."

Panic swelled-
as a gland of stars dissolved
there was no answer
of mechanism to the menace.

I was in the tunnel of a forest
pressed against a door-
the woods thronged with holes
that howled feral trills
and the alarms sounded
as animals crawled on transparent talons
onto the ceiling of the skyline of brass thorns

***

Once
      I tried to throw away
the book the anchoress wrote-
    as dictated to her by a priest.

I could no longer
stomach the violence-
       and I rejected mythology
             as it enveloped and devoured me.
Then my light impaled the snow-
      and struggled free;
for I knew the sounds of escape so well.

I knew I would no longer go with the deer hunter-
    and his demands to pull the trigger.

    ***

What I cannot say or explain-
            belongs to the Iuk Kide.
And when I am behind the door- and the woods leer
    I hear the shackles
        along the bottoms of the glass rivers-
      and when they crack you can see the soil
        break through- full of teeth

Briefly I wanted
    To try and be holy-

I put a plate of oranges out into the sun;

    I created a dark surface with water
    so that the moths would come.

I knew of others who did the same;
but they had killing jars-
and would crucify them
while chanting Latin.

I wanted to watch a moth's tiny membrane of a wing
come to a glass of water-
which falls over because it is possessed
by something other than water.
***

The western world follows us everywhere.
I am never close to it-
because it is there all of the time.
I hear the narrative of hunters.

It is not a coincidence-
the patterns and the option of madness-

See the queen in the ceremony.

The commoners spread around her
And sing in chorus:

"Everyone in the world loves a happy graveyard.
Everyone in the world loves a dying queen."

Her face began to crack
as stone and her whole body
shattered to the ground.

molecular: /məlɛkjələr/

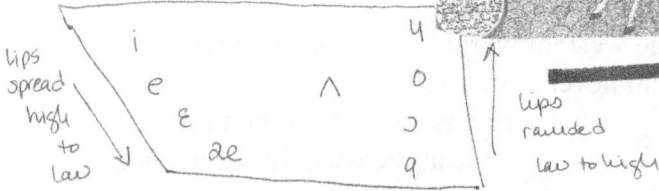

The cardinal vowels

lips
spread
high
to
low

i   ɥ
  e   ʌ   o
    ɛ   ɔ
      æ   ɑ

lips
rounded
low to high

front vowels:
lips spreading

Back vowels:
lips rounded

lengthy discussion
/lɜŋgθi dĭskʌsən/

After this happened-
        I looked at diagrams of queen insects inside the
                    king's hall...

and realized that the last thing she had written was her
belief : *the queen is in fact the slave...*

        I wept for her death and found solace in the
                    anchoress.

                    ***

      The mother of the anchoress
        had had many lovers.

        She had been the one
                the only
                the other
                and the forgotten.
        She decided that there had been
              too many messages thrown- and
        she did not want to drown.

She left her daughter to the priests and disappeared.

        Guilt seemed to be
        the only simulation of an option outside of her
                    condition.

The mother thought that there was something wrong her-

she blamed herself-
for all that she did and all that she did not.

As a child the anchoress grew out her hair-
to keep out the cold.
She learned how to talk properly- and not to look into
the eyes of strangers

Once her mother lived by the ocean
and would tie her legs together underwater.

The anchoress prayed to god
and whispered to me while I was asleep-

until I wrote of the ocean.

The repetition which occurs is accidental
and acts as a wax collecting on top of itself
into the palm of her half-open hand.

The Theory of Transgenerational Haunting:

*The idea that repressed secrets are passed from
One generation to the next in encrypted form.*

The first thing I remember

since being alive is when I was a child
I sat up in bed
while looking through the open door
and thought:
"This will be my first memory"

Twenty years later-
in a dream
a man told me that he did not know I was a wom-
an until I opened my mouth…

I went to the mirror
and opened my mouth
to see the origin of what made me female-

but I woke up.

Dyirbal Gender Classes

Class I: human males; storms; the moon; most
snakes; fishes; insects;
some birds.

Class II: human females; the sun and the stars;
anything connected
with fire and water; dogs; harmful fishes;
some snakes;
most birds and most weapons.

Class III: Edible fruit and the trees that bear them.

Class IV: Body parts, meat, bees and honey; wind;
most trees;
grass; mud and stones… …

A walled garden clad in ashes.
The flight of a butterfly signifying death.

Deer shedding their antlers to grow new ones.
Roses planted to attract nightingales.

Abandoned thermal fields and solar farms.
Eelgrass meadows with nocturnal glass eyes.

Shallow sounds and open water.

Dyirbal Gender Classes:
 Women, Fire, and Dangerous Things

Class I : human males; storms; moon;
 most snakes; fishes; insects;
 some birds

Class II : human females; sun + stars;
 anything connected with fire + water,
 dogs; harmful fish; some snakes;
 most birds; most weapons

Class III : Edible fruit and trees that bear them

Class IV : Body parts, meat, bees + honey
 wind, most trees, grass, mud, stones

МОРСКІЯ СИРЕНЫ.

***

The corruption of bodies occurring as accidents of
                                                    motion-
            universes of other universes
                        shorn and smoldering
            from heat, pressure and other means…

the softer rock cuts away from the harder
            forms a single span
grows hayfields and timberlines
                        blooms yucca's and choke cherries
to escape the delay and undertow-
            to negate a carapace-

measuring what is know in song cycles of momentum-
                                        of dreamings.

        The dreamings acting as a boat I use-
        poling across
        water tinted amber
                    to the inner reaches of a pond
                                as a prairie
                                        made by peat fire.
        Extending the outcroppings of possibilities-
                    imaginary etchings
        to ease the application of a ritual life.

The simulation of a violin maker
who studies trees
and then sharpens their branches
outside of her house

so they can lean into enemies.

"What I believe in is what I mean."
-gertrude stein

Brief errors in transition timing.

I see the moorland
The farmland
The badlands

The ghost forest
The climax forest.

Calculate your position.

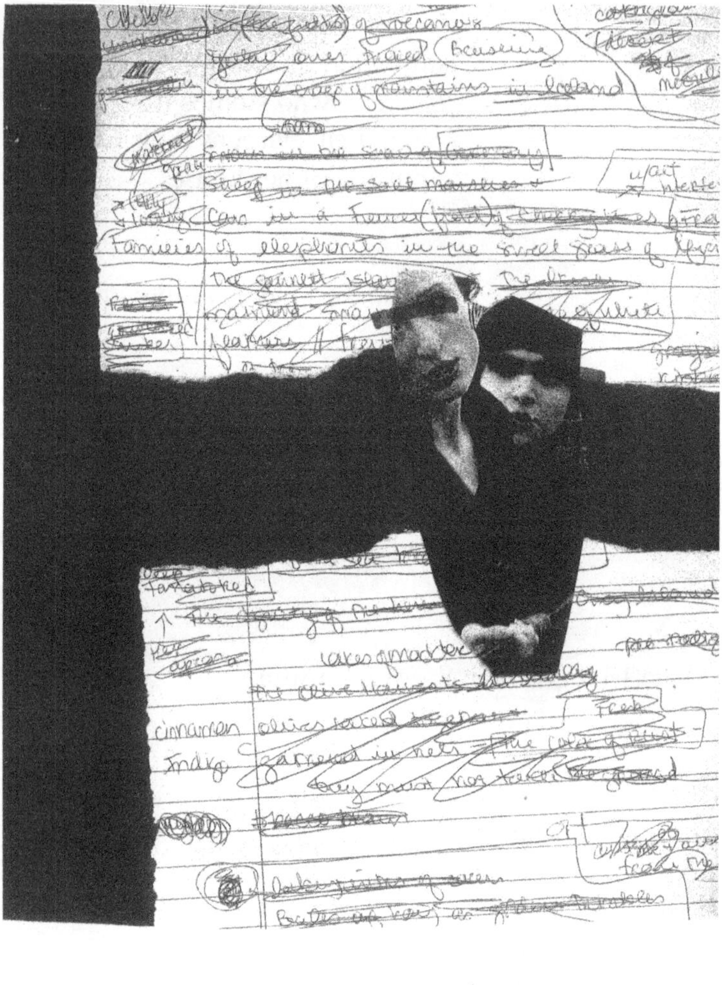

cinnamon
Indigo

NIGHT BABY, FRAGMENTS:
2009

Night Baby

crumb of grace
the hearse of one's heart outside, plumbing the outlaw
                                                    seeds

my bird stomach and apple face of moat and temperate

rush, gush, and gish
feckless
to bed and to bed
a glamorous grammar

abyss in a flower vase.

ghost darling
shared chromosome or a shared cave

Blind patients — hallucinations of sight.

ungulates — hoofed animals

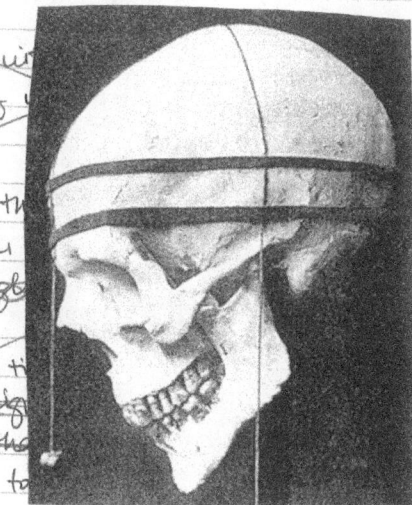

I battle wi~~
as if ~~

I think th~~
when ~~
though~~

After that ~~
~~
~~
~~
to rebuild.

I believe
that my words can be powerful —
that they have the ability to cripple.
That is why I do not always tell her
when she hurts me...

Night Baby

we are perfect twins
with matching sins and fingerprints

little bones
    little bones in the trees

little bones
    in my watch

little bones among the bees.

Night Baby

when we talk
we don't talk at all

something happens
slight and succinct
as carapace
as a fall place

even in person
ripple and thaw

our skulls become special

our skulls overwhelm everything.

Night Baby

gusto
    both bride and husband
gunslinger of the Midwest
    author, canary
    not Margaret.

under spell
    silver
        and sailor
            wilderness.

free from approval and rejection
    a look of a walk

crypt borders
    find me
        but retain your holy.

...w is the
a pain
bicycles bu...
against the

eyes addressi...
a bue...
a ...

to the sea,   silver
lips busts   reeds

light as ...
the ec...

Like Jesus, Dionysus and Osiris were be-
trayed by trusted companions, suffered
deaths involving severe mutilation and spent
some time in the Underworld before being
resurrected to take an important place in the
affairs of heaven.

fingers ...
fingers ...
knees ...

our thin ...
in the sh...
he...
below the

ing the piano
...ly touch.

...eet lights
...d
...e cold sun.

Night Baby

sexy pants
dollmaker
    lets play a game
    with no machines

swagger
    knife-love
with the messages of fingertips

memory
    you wound me like a squid.

Night Baby

today
design and dark

a piano inside of an empty bar

everything outside:
wood and coal
children and widows

a scream in the shower
a scream on the bus
a scream in the movie theater

WITCH FIRE:
2009-2010

Witch Fire: Mother and Daughter

1.
My daughter's hair is so dark
it washes her face, slakes gardens.
Mouth of sunlight.

Mother this and mother that.
She was never mine.
She was formed in the fates before I arrived.

Severe as a soldier.
Gentle as cornfields.

It wasn't my choice.
She lived before me,
She gave birth to me
so I could give birth to her.

2.
Starched dress.
Crisp black bonnet.

Time changes the weather,
alters the light.

The bonnet is too close to her face.
I want to loosen the ribbons.

She says "My name is Anne,"
and then "My name is Elizabeth."

Her eyes keep changing,
blue, brown, gray, and then green.

Her figure is an empty house.
Her hands are small orphans.

She is motherless,
she is singular and clean.
She is unhurried and tall
against the swamps and the chickens.

3.
My quiet child in the countryside.

Eyes of a psychic.

Wildflowers burn as compasses, create too many
                                        suns.
We are too simple here.
stirrings on the sea.

little egg.
little whale that has lost its way.

water of the womb.
my half-open purse.

heartbeat inside
like the wings of a paper swan.

4.
When your father left
I sat by the window.

You were a baby lying in the crib he painted
white.

When he left that day
you slept
and the pots and pans rattled in the cabinets
and the sheets raised off of the bed

but I didn't notice
because I was waiting for him
to change his mind and come back.

5.
Newborn,
smudged in blood
then wiped clean
given pink mittens

suckling and tagged.

Is it true,
that one day
you will be someone's bride?

6.
Knowing her
is a nameless thing.

It grows in the grass,
in the sky, and in the sea.
Marsh hawks and sail fish, too, have children
and yet, I understand nothing.
Nature brings me no closer.

It is not unusual.
It is in the tulips and swarms of bees.
It is in everything

and yet,
it is fresh,
and persisting.

The octopus, the antelope, and the locust.

All of it budding, gorged,
and infinite.

Beauty is larger than logic.

7.
To be a mother
is a silent film

and I was an actress
with a pearl-lined womb.

I carried her, unborn,
like a rare fossil

and the world became watchful
with a sibilant touch.

Under the eyes of strangers
I bloomed,
pagan and unashamed,

her noise inside
louder than witch-fire.

Starched dress
crisp black bonnett

time changes the weather
alters the light

the bonnett is too close to her face
I want to loosen the ribbons

She
an

He
bu

Her
Her

Salem witchcraft.

She
She is singular + clean.

She is unhurried + tall
against the swamp + the chickens

LETHE:
Post-Modern Tales of the Urban Underworld, Fragments, 2011-2012

Phonetics ▬▬▬▬▬▬ Phonology

concrete   abstract

continuous   ▬▬▬   discrete

speech processing signal ▬▬ Language representation
                                            and
                                            rules

speech processing
    has s[...]

language rep[...]

θ think, though
j you, univers[...]

tʃ church, witch

ŋ ring, anger

ɾ letter, bitter

voice /vɔɪs/
tide /taɪd/
ground /graʊnd/

think /θɪŋk/
that /ðæt⁷/

concentrate /kɑnsɪntret/

above /əbʌv/

~~woman/wimin~~

women /wɪmɪn/

LETHE
Lethe: Rewritten (Post-Modern Tales of the Urban Underworld)

Madame Gorgon.
Slither, stitch and hiss.
Tiny eyes turn black in candlelight, a fever pitch.
Deformed queen of the back room, scaled and hoofed.
She knows what men want.
She has been all over the world.
Nose of a bat, speaking every human language.
The smell of animal bones found in bogs and swamps

and the centaurs are underground scholars
sharing their libraries with the secret elect
leading the way on slender haunches

everything trembles
the dance begins
and the wings unfold
only dry breaths of wind tunnel like with a half-cupped
                                                    hand to the ear

An ache in the ache of it.
A touch in the touch of it.

Again the need for touch and quiet.
Again, each small unnamable thing.

A granule, a spark, a flash.

Another list to tide the tide of time.

Another heart to hear a heart.

A world of facts.
Each bone holds itself in place.
Gravity makes the snow fall from the tree branches

and the earth must tilt just so to be on good terms with
                                                        the sun.

I see the future in the past.

silhouettes
gestures
grace
downcast

The state of betweeness knows sunlight and
underwater
darkness and nothingness and everything.

A calm and breathless perspective:
a vision of planetary dust and ash,
the cool sigh of infinite bones

ADA'S DREAMS:
2013-2014

зоему.   Happy families

мешалось в доме Облонских.

ранцуженкою-гувернанткой, и объявила

оложение это продолжалось уже третий день и мучительно чувствова... и сам

ругами, и всеми членами семьи, и домочадцами. Все члены семьи и

ствовали, что нет смысла в их сожительстве и что на каждом постоялом дворе

учайно сошедшиеся люди более связаны между собой, чем они, члены семьи и

мочадцы Облонских. Жена не выходила из своих комнат, мужа третий день не б

ма. Дети бегали по всему дому, как потерянные; англичанка поссорилась с эконо

исала записку приятельнице, прося приискать ей новое место; повар ушел еще

ра, во время обеда; черная кухарка и кучер просили расчета. На третий день пос

ры князь Степан Аркадьич Облонский - Стива, как его звали в свете, - в обычны

есть в восемь часов утра, проснулся не в спальне жены, а в своем кабинете, на

ьянном диване.. Он повернул свое полное, выхоленное тело на пружинах диван

желая опять заснуть надолго, с другой стороны крепко обнял подушку и прижал

щекой; но вдруг вскочил, сел на диван и открыл крепко глаза. Да, да, как это было? - ду

споминая сон. - Да, как это было? Да! Алабин давал обед в П

штадте, а что-то американское. Да,

обед на стеклянных столах, да, - и с

ще, и какие-то маленькие графинчи

Степана Аркадьича весело заблесте

орошо. Много еще там было отлич

е выразишь". И, заметив полосу све

н весело скинул ноги с дивана, отыс

ния в прошлом году), обделанные в зо

илетней привычке, не вставая, потянул

И тут он вспомнил вдруг, как и

в с его лица, он смор

Ada's Dreams: Distant Future Visions

An ink sketch of planets revolving around the sun
A white woman crying in an enormous black velvet dress,
        kneeling in a gilded cathedral
The pungent nose-burning odor of salted fish
Cold water over aching arms covered by boils and burns
Senses trapped like an endangered bird, stories as feelings, a
       field of bright blue unblinking eyes

The fragrant ghost breath of lotus flower ponds
Cherry blossoms fall and fill the streets like snow
A supernova shines from the constellation Ophiuchus
Deities of Earth blink from their numerous shines, and the
        priestess shakes

The dark bulls are fighting in a meadow, and there are
        people cheering
in the smell of manure and common blue wildflowers
Twelve goddesses dance, a triptych of feathers and colored
        paper on wood

The imperial court bones sleep and awake, sleep and awake
The trade of pepper, cowry shells, porcelain and slaves
The plague spreads among the faces of friends and family
  The infected are sent to live in cabins outside of the
      village, rotting from the inside out

A wedding, a rape, a death, a birth, the funeral

      (know I have clean hands and a clean heart)

Good and bad quartos, golden coins and madrigals

The passions of young shepherds and their mistresses in the

                                  fields

      What is crying? I cannot remember the feeling.

      (Sweet Helen, make me immortal with a kiss.)

    Desideratum, Erase

        Evomit adsorptum eaeco de gutture cetus;
        Redditure terrae qui modo praeda fuit

`¥ qæ o^l wɘl Y{ ^ℚ,[ɮɮ̄ mê≤ wɘ≤ z'ƙ tℚ

qƨy sɯ [ɮɮi `{ `ɣ,ℚw qæpƙ 1xØ Yæ qꭤ

        vis electrica

        a prima mundi origine deducti

        دَوْلَتِ عَلِيَّهْ عُثْمَانِيَّهْ

                 La

            Grandeza Mexi-

            cana

                Von
            Romeo undth
            Julitha
        Mbudye… Kalala

Ilunga… Kasala…Nkole

      Век живи́ — век учи́сь

ukiyo zoshi

banovi
עברb
distinctio rationis
ratiocinatae

Skeleton Man

My beast is to be fed every night, more than other people's
                                                    beasts.
I begin to see the skeletons inside of people while they
                                        laugh in the city park
or stand stiff faced with boredom in banks and grocery
                                                    stores.

              I wake up thinking about drones. I wake up thinking
                                              about poverty.
              I wake up thinking about my own death.
              I am a man obsessed with death.
              I dream of the universe, but it is not the universe.
               It is the sweeping after-image of a starless city sky.

Dear Universe:
What are your true origins? Are your secrets visible?
Out of the bones of recorded history, violence appears
                                          inevitable.

The Floating World (madness)

: A history

IMAGES white light:
flashes of sanity

Wrist-banging, procession and howling

SCRIPT/MONOLOGUE/DIALOGUE

...I have woken up from a long emotional sleep.

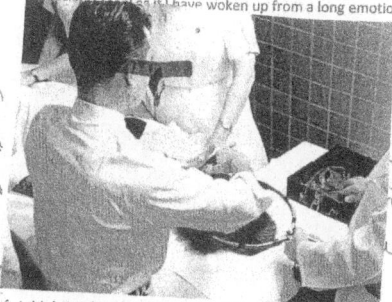

...reams, sex, a book, a song, or a work

I think I realize that it's over, and then I realize that it's just not looking me in the face

I close my eyes against the light

Hoping to wake up as someone else

A person who made different decisions

A woman who didn't open the door.

group throwing papers in the air

drinking glasses of water

umbrellas (procession)

woman with bird cage

duck, duck, goose

gurney strapped

white balloon

up + down the stair case

hiii?"

free standing door (a platform)

free standing staircase

tall glasses water

chair of leaves (paper)

rocking back & forth

cabinet of pill

Borderland

The stars are changing, we look for them, argue about their
location

People take turns speaking in different languages, but they
still have the same questions

The children pretend to be trees; they stand very still and
hold branches

The dream continues, the glimpse of the divine disorients

Before birth, souls wandering as feelings

I went into the shadow world and died

My angel whispers to me: *don't turn away*

Visions from the Borderland (mortality/universe)

(hands over eyes)
a group of widows
(black dresses)

IMAGES

Projected images of the universe

Stars changing in sky as if an observatory, individuals looking for the stars, arguing about location

Scientists arguing about the origin of the universe

graveyard
wheelchair

People taking turns speaking different languages

Flowers given to the audience

People as trees, holding branches

white gowns / white hats

white chalk
make-up

SCRIPT/MONOLOGUE/DIALOGUE

Have I dreamed my life?

A glimpse of the divine disorients

" I went to the shadow world and died."

"Blood is still on the knife"

" Before birth, we were born, we wandered here as a feeling "

" Don't turn away "

white painted
fish nets

white
muslin

Set (s) (rolling platforms)

white
muslin

white painted

white sheet

91

The Floating World: Madness

1.

Women are vomiting their food, they are dying in
hospitals,

they are banging their illiterate wrists and heads

in an endless child bride procession

in an endless abortion

ii.

She closes her eyes to the light

She hopes to wake up as someone else

A person who made different decisions

A woman who didn't open the door.

(You hold the rifle like this)

I was born near the gray lands of desert farms
and low lapping gray water.

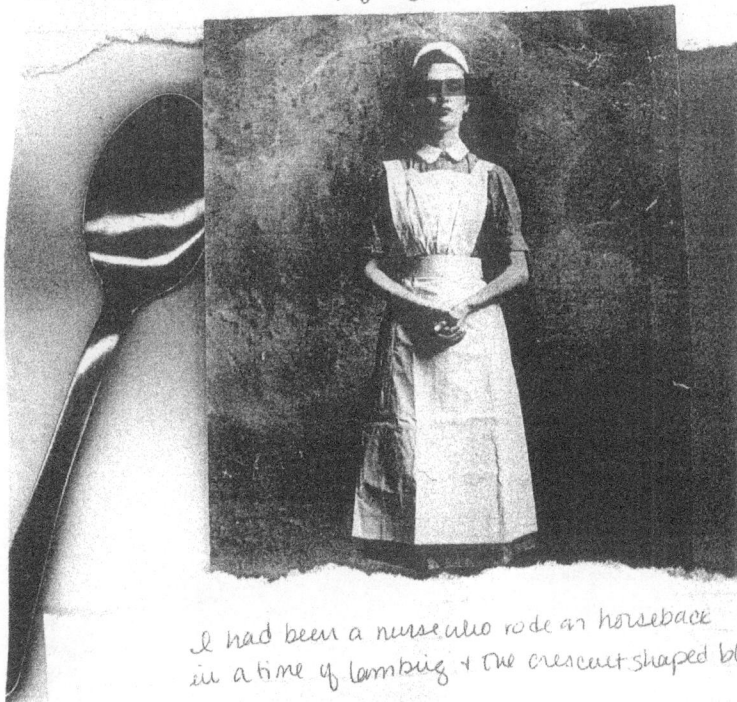

I had been a nurse who rode on horseback
in a time of lambing + the crescent shaped bl

THE APPLE IN THE GRASS (romantic love)

Images:

A couple is in a boat, ~~they are wearing all white~~, rowing in place, ~~snow is falling and the screen behind them is dimly illuminated gray.~~ *Red*

Eating fruit / *Bowls of fruit*  *flower wreaths/head*

Throwing red flower petals

Washing face from bowls of water

Smoking cigarettes at the edge of the ocean

Dancing

Prayer

A parade of wedding dresses

Walking through an empty mirror

growing up on toilet, repeating their name over and over

der blanket in darkness

no in the dark

oung male snorts cocaine

Woods projected image screen

Love letters are given to the audience

Eros / Dionysus

ocean (sheet)

The Apple in the Grass: Western Romantic Love

A couple is in a boat, they are wearing all white,
rowing the boat in place
Gold ornaments, gold leaves and gold foil tilting
towards the sun
a place where it is always autumn
The audience is feral and watching from the woods
the silver screen behind them is dimly illuminated gray
They are eating fruit and throwing red flower petals

A chorus sings: I love you always and still

A chorus sings: Every morning light comes through the
window

They are washing their faces in bowls of clean water and
smoking cigarettes
They dance and they pray, they walk through an empty
mirror

I, ENGINE:
2014-2015

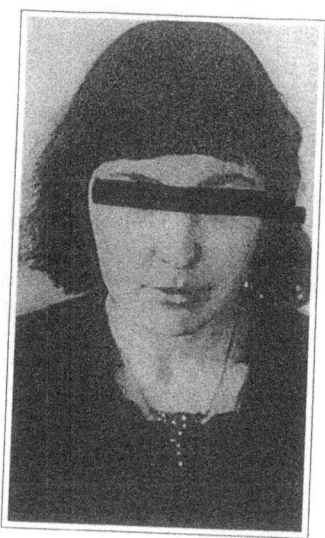

Marina Tsvetaeva

Marina Ts

Before the Rev
the publicati
ute of a sma
a St. Petersburg lite
her home in Mosc
imperial capital, w
Moscow," she repo
the author of a vol
spontaneity and u
published herself,
summarily dismisse
awkwardness and
mand
row he
cultiva
l extre

The Etherial Retriever
a pinhole focused on the fragment
of white light, grassey cells + moonset.

I, Engine

I, Engine.
I , Echo.
I, Erase.
The eternal return.
A pinhole focused on a fragment of white light, gnashing
                                        cells, and moon set.
Confronting the shadow and waking up in another dream.
The bird of darkness sings.

Basilisk, cockatrice and sphinx.
A restless tide of telepathy
the immortal will to burn a hole
to carve a fragile space
for my one grain of sand.

I, Engine
In a moment
End squalor under.
Inside the belly of a shark, a mechanism of muscle, fossil
ancient winter and its cold meat
drones flutter blue skies gifting shrapnel
killing clenches at utmost unspeak
to crush and to suffer a fast and a fever, farewells of the
forever funeral.

I, Engine
Head sloped for forgiveness.
Windows weep and the smell of burning.
My eye is the thimble.

I, Forge
I, Embark
I, Resolve
Becoming the seeds of Summerland
embedded in the golden and blooded threads of Akashic
Records.

the heart beats for only so long
traveling slowly while covered in the dust of stars.

I, Organ
I, Lung
I, Egg
Mammal suckling the chrysalis of pale chromosomal milk
A thick sluice and mossy soup of infinitesimal splits,
                inchoate rhythms, and pulpy decompositions.

I, River
I, Emerge
I, Endure
my body is over
in a moment of candle, snow, and branches.
to belong and to begin, briefly, I live.

10-1-14

~~synaptic cloud hung and uncharted~~
~~water with its obsidian, its cold meat~~

domes flutter (as in the) blue skies
gifting schrapnel

~~killing clenches at utmost with unspeak~~

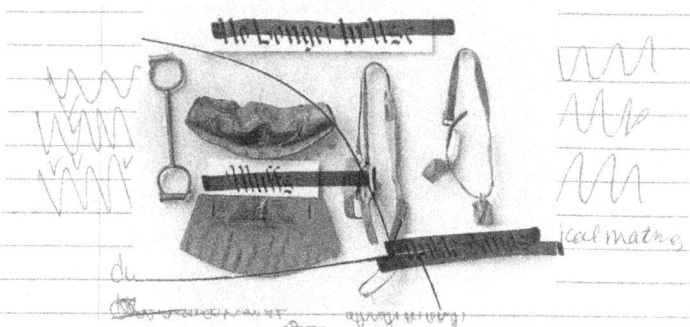

fall and ~~[crossed out]~~ fire goes bombastic
~~[crossed out]~~ tinder, the blood and rust
of constant kings

to crush & to suffer a fast + fever, the
~~farewell~~ of a forever funeral

101